Teen
Whispering

To Judy & Rob!

Love,
Rays

Teen Whispering

A WAY FOR PARENTS TO
"GET THROUGH IT"

———

Jon K. Amundson, Ph.D.

Copyright © 2016 Jon K. Amundson, Ph.D.
All rights reserved.

ISBN: 1533217874
ISBN 13: 9781533217875

Introduction

A PARENT ONCE SAID TO me regarding his normal but spirited son that he was "not sure [he] would get through it," meaning the five to seven years of his son's adolescence. Hence the title of this short but focused book on teens, parents, and survival. While short and simple, the material here is not fast food. Most parenting books try to hook the reader with promises regarding how quickly the application of their techniques will lead to getting kids to listen and parents in the driver's seat. While the ideas in self-help books are often simple, they bypass the central and most important element. That element is the focus upon parents *and* their state of mind: the yoga of teen parenting!

To run a marathon, you need to train. The same is true to play the piano, get the most out of your computer, or do woodwork. Simple techniques are best applied when the right conditioning, practice, training, or tool-use preparation has taken place. So we start with the adult, the parent, as the key to the situation you want with your teen.

CHAPTER 1

Simple but Not Easy

Before launching into any coaching, I have to say some folks will not be able to do it. By "do it" I refer to mastering the skills and state of mind necessary to make things work better. There are two factors that promise success or failure in any attempt toward better parenting generally. The first is aptitude.

Aptitude

By "aptitude" I reference the basic, fundamental capacity to manage one's state of mind. A kid can, if predisposed, be only a little calmer than his or her most agitated parent. So capacity or aptitude to address one's (adult) state of mind relative to general agitation or reactive agitation in a child needs to be the first consideration before you bother with reading any further.

Adults with a history of significant agitation, distraction, internal focus, disinterest, or problems in self-management, social presence, and relationships aren't going to get as much out of these ideas as those not so predisposed. Or they will have to work harder!

The second issue is exceptionality.

Exceptionality

By "exceptionality" I am referring to conditions where a teen is *significantly* challenged by a developmental, conduct, or anxiety and mood disorder. The self-help orientation here has limits with the truly challenged. Though in fact the same principles are applied with autism spectrum disorders, conduct disorders, oppositional defiant disorder, or mood and anxiety disorders in youths, it is just a little harder outside of the consulting room and with a book to do as much as quickly. With these kids you'll have to work even harder.

With this in mind, let's talk about making a difference, but that difference starts with you.

CHAPTER 2

If You Can't Bring It, You Can't Do It

WE WILL SPEAK A LOT about teens and their social and developmental challenges, but there is no use going there without you going somewhere first. As mentioned, a kid can only self-regulate or downregulate to the same degree a parent can, and so we are talking about modelling calm(er) as your basic state of mind.

By "state of mind" I refer to a parent's underlying capacity to self-regulate, to be able to think about thinking and then be responsive effectively to the circumstances of his or her life. Much of our actions/reactions are habitual, meaning regulated by patterns, expectations, and routine. Habit creates state of mind, such as driving your car on a Saturday, when you don't need to go to work but you unconsciously make the "work turn" anyway.

What do I mean then by "state of mind" relative to teen whispering? Let's look at this negative example:

> Round 1: Teen's mom wants the kid to turn off the computer and go to bed, come to dinner, help with chores, do homework, and so on. So she says, "Irwin, please turn off the computer." Irwin somnambulantly mutters agreement, and the teen's mom goes away with a sense of either self-approbation for her calm civility or mild dread for noncompliance.
> Round 2: You guessed it! Kid is still in thrall to the screen, and the teen's mom reminds him with a slightly more expansive admonition that "this is the second time" or that he "can do it later" or the reason(s) he "ought to be more responsible," and so on. And you know what is coming…
> Round 3: The teen's mom gets to cash in all her points for patience, civility, and calm demeanor, and we end up off to the races.

Over the years I have had parents do everything from literally cutting the cord to the electrical distraction to dealing physical violence. But let's get scientific about this.

As a basis to understanding the principles that follow and will serve as your training protocol, let's look at how all parents of teens and teens themselves go to hell. This can be represented in the following graph:

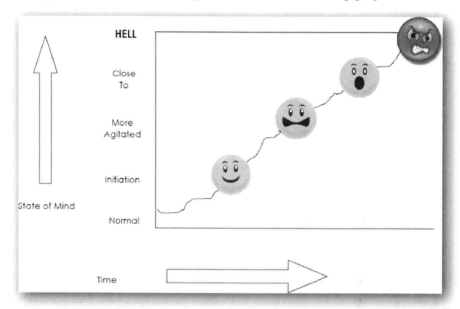

Our time series represents the escalating failure associated with our example. At time series #1, there is brief intrusive instruction often accompanied by anxious trepidation regarding failure to secure compliance. Then there is a second or third effort, all escalating in agitation and generally of a bilateral nature, involving both the kid and the parent. The algorithmic curve runs fast at the end, and we call #4 hell. The issue of the computer, in our example, may now be supplanted by issues related to parental unfairness, the teen's lack of respect, conflict over responsibility, why the teen's mom likes a sibling more, how much the mom has done for the teen, gratitude, reciprocity, authority, and so on, but mostly nonsense that has a latency of its own. People are in hell for longer or shorter periods of time depending upon their capacity for tolerating strong emotions.

In addition, this curve can run faster or slower depending upon the agitation load of a parent or a kid. The more agitation on board circumstantially or in one's nature, boom! The quicker you go to hell.

Got it? So what then are the central training principles and the ways/means for a parent to use this information and go to hell a little less often?

CHAPTER 3

How Not to Go to Hell, or at Least Less Often and for a Shorter Time

Jon K. Amundson, Ph.D.

Periods of Time
The first word I will try to operationalize for you is "patience."

Patience
If I had a dollar for every time a parent has said, "But I am patient," I would retired, and rich. The truth is if you are in my office or reading this book, what you call "patience" isn't. In surveys everyone rates himself or herself as "pretty fit, and in good health too," and every man over fifty thinks he's about 100 percent tougher than he is. Patience too is unduly self-attributed and not at all what it needs to be. By patience I mean the ability to

- downregulate urgency,
- use the physiological and cognitive braking system we all possess and underemploy, and
- find a calming pleasure in being criticized, corrected, and evaluated, if not hated, by your teen!

Most parents define patience as "I was nicer than I needed to be for a few minutes before I could treat them the way they deserve." While I cannot show you here the way patience feels, you can experiment with it by using the following cognitive prods. By "prods" I mean bumper stickers, quick sayings that evoke a better state of mind. This points to the essence of patience, or the path to the foundation needed to get through life with your teen. Ready?

First, "Urgency is not my friend." What does this mean? Well, we live a fast-food life and feed our kids and loved ones a lot of hurry up, get it done, move it along, and on to the next thing. If you want to parent more effectively at any age, urgency is to good parenting what high fat, sugar, and salt are to a healthy diet.

Second, "I cannot afford to lose my mind (and/or go to hell) for this one or anyone." Patience is prophylaxis to loss of mind, and loss of mind is the death knell of patience. Most of us were raised and taught what the hell: if provoked, if they act this or that way, it's fair game to default to anger or to throw up our arms and collapse or to run to pathos or a similar strong emotion. Then we may get compliance (anxious or surly submission), maybe sympathy ("oh, poor you"), or even a free ticket to emotional collapse ("what I have to bear"). So give up losing your mind; know that it is a failure of patience and that going to hell is *always* an option. One error, and you are on the road.

Third, "Well, I either go where they live or stay where I live and maybe they'll come over here." They will either succumb to your state of mind—that is, respond to your patience and the resulting authority (see below)—or you will fall to theirs. However, if they sway you, you begin to hear that voice that says:

- They have to listen!
- Who are they to speak to me that way!
- By God I shall not put up with this!
- Only one of us is gonna be in charge here!

Finally, patience is furthered by a degree of benign tolerance or adequate challenge, so to use our last prompt, it is useful to understand, for now, and maybe going forward, this kid is gonna be a challenge, but you gotta love it!

The downstream consequence of the practice of patience is authority—a cornerstone to managing a teen. No, not authority over him or her but authority over yourself!

Coda

I wish I could take credit for this summary, but in fact what follows was mined from the Internet and has been repeated there. It captures the essence of the ideas here, and it is the *CTFD approach* I advocate for parenting generally and for teens especially. CTFD?

Calm the f*** down!

CHAPTER 4

The Biopsychosocial Teen World and CTFD

THE TRADITIONAL IMAGE OF TEENS and their contrariness is accurate, and not. Let me explain this situation. I have used the term "biopsychosocial" here to speak to the three layers of teen-ness, so to speak. First, from the onset of puberty to the early twenties, there are interesting things happening to a teen at the level of the nervous and endocrine systems. There is a lot of biological stuff going on, so the old expression "It's the hormones" is not without consideration. The best way to think about this is that the battle for identity—Who am I? What are these other people in my world about? And where am I going?—leads to cellular battles. The basic limits of the brain are developing and linking up as the teen is thinking and acting in the world. "Battle" is used because experience gets the neurons—those basic units—into competition. One set-up of habit/thought/behavior means other habits/thoughts/behaviors aren't being set up. Let me use a pretty simple example:

> Question: Why do we not want youths/teens to smoke?
> Answer: The potentiating of the nicotinic receptors in the brain.

This means that a nicotine habit that can be established at the level of the nervous system in the teen years is almost unknown to be established after the age of twenty-five! Too late, the brain has other things it is dedicated to, and those pathways to nicotine dependence are lost, for the most part.

So at this biological level, there is articulation, branching, and pruning going on as the system is awash in hormonal changes. As mentioned, however, there are the fundamental questions regarding who I will be / what shall I be about in relation to others / where I shall go: the psychological component.

Identity is the answer to these questions as each teen strives for his or her own agency or presence or impact upon his or her world. Boys and girls go about this differently, but as they move from the bubble of the family world toward the bubble of their own world, each will have to negotiate this demand:

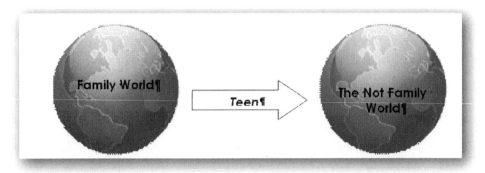

How I will be, who I will be with, how I will be noticed and fit in, what I will value, and how I will do things, manage challenges, find my way, and so on are the essential challenges. The mandate then for the teen is this:

> You must practice your life and go into the world, but that will be possible only to the extent you manage your family, until you leave home.

The *social context* is the largest context within which to consider our teens. Let's go back to the first sentence in this chapter about teen contrariness and why it is and is not true. The not-true relates to other cultures and social settings where teens are not considered a problem. The things we wrestle with here are not so there. I was speaking with a friend from Kenya and teased him about how I was sure he too, like the youths he now worked with in North America, talked back, had trouble getting up for school, didn't help around the house, and so on, and he was horrified! Nothing like that would ever happen as the social and cultural expectations in his teen years were so well set, and opportunity so limited, rebellion had no room.

So there is the simple answer—that where the past, the present and the future are more stable and predictable and serve as protective authority, or the larger society/culture is cohesive and regular, teens do better, hormones be damned. "Protective authority" is a useful term. When traditions exist in the form of values, limits, and expectations therein, things go better for kids in families and people in society. As is pretty obvious in the larger world today, in North America the holding and protective traditions are, to say the least, ephemeral:

- Most of us don't live in proximity to our families of origin or other first-degree relatives.
- Most of us have enjoyed or suffered at least two significant loves in our adult lives.
- Many of us will see, actually or virtually, each day more people than our great-grandparents saw in a lifetime.
- A vast majority of North Americans have changed their religion at least once in their lifetimes.
- Not to mention the acceleration of technology and exposure to the world on the Internet and in cyberspace (for example, the average age of exposure to explicit adult sexuality is eleven).

The fixed aspect of the social world for the last seventy-five years is more in flux than fixed, and the cost is less protective authority outside the family for our kids.

Finally, and most importantly, how you see your teen will also dictate how you manage each other. In fact, your teen is the most energized, creative, excited, and expansive he or she will ever be. Teens are indigenous philosophers and lawyers. They are in the throes of eye-opening experiences never to be repeated. Their inner genius is engaged and ready to go, and if we can see that they are full of this energy, we can appreciate them, even love them, even in their most conflicted moments. They, like a Nobel Prize winner, are just working it out, and if we listen, use the formula (see below), and even offer appreciation, we do get through it better.

CHAPTER 5
Into the Breach

When I was in the Peace Corps, prior to going in-country, we were inoculated against every disease you could get inoculated for. Consider what you have covered so far in your inoculation in preparation for going in-country. If you don't feel your immune system is there yet, reread and even consider getting a personal trainer (therapist) to get you into shape.

What we are speaking about at this point is engagement.

Engagement

What I mean by "engagement" is a generic skill to connect, set up some communication, and exercise influence. To understand this, let's use some more letters (without the profanity).

C/R/D

The first letter is for "calm." Not much can get done if there is not some calm called forth when it comes to teens and teen moments. OK, calm might better be called calmer or calm enough, and again, like patience, most of the calming step is left up to you. Patience is to calm what sunshine is to a flower, or music to a dancer, or a fly to a trout, but you get my drift. Calm is the induction of a state of mind in the teen necessary for any further influence. Calm is linked intimately, and recursively, to our next letter, *R* for "receptivity," each intimately related to the other, two sides of the same coin. But let's stay with calm a little longer.

Calm is the ability to model not only patience but authority in the face of an invitation to lose one's mind—remember our diagram?—to hold on to a little bit of solidness even at the most challenging moments. For some of us, this will be through enhanced verbal communication, and for others, a beautiful yet powerful silence. Cut to scene 1.

> Scene 1
> While being indicted for unfairness, poverty of proper parenting, or lack of responsiveness to precocious demands, we see a parent

simply holding on to a position with no rush to get out of the room and all the (apparent) time in the world to continue to invite the teen to express himself or herself in a manner consistent with calm(er) articulation!

So, how to get there? Initially calm has to do with focus upon process, not content. S/he who controls process rules the world, sort of. But what do we mean by process versus content? Cut to scene 2.

> Scene 2
> Parent: Hey, time to get up and get ready for school.
> Teen: I *said* I would!
> Parent: You always say "just a minute" or you are going to do it and never do! So how am I supposed to believe this time is any different, and I need you to do it right now, and so on.

All right, we can perhaps see where this is going, but as the teen fulminates and cranks up his agitation, we cut to scene 3, where the parent uses the "all the time / no hurry to get out of the room" approach.

> Scene 3
> Teen: I said I'd get up!
> Parent: I'm sorry, I need you to do that now.
> Teen: (Silence)
> Parent: Excuse me. Can you get up now?
> Teen: Just leave me alone!
> Parent: Hey, I'm sorry about this, but I do need you to get up.

Recycle to effect.

What you can't see in this exchange is the parent dropping his or her shoulders, evoking the calmest demeanor possible, and finding pleasure in the interaction. Also there is no shift in conversation to content not related to "get up." Each cycle, the parent must use the old admonition that

> successful parenting of a teen consists of finding pleasure in being held in contemptuously low opinion by the object of your affection/attention.

The central tenet of calm then is that either the teen will take you to where he or she lives—feelings of being underappreciated, pushed around, not respected, angry, and so on—or you will bring him or her to where you should be—reasonably able to hold on to your own calm if not humorous sense of authority regarding the issue of the moment. Let's get to R to continue unpacking this.

R, as mentioned, is for "receptivity." If you've ever bought something you didn't even know you were shopping for, you've been "receptivitized." In the equation, you see that

$$(C \leftarrow \rightarrow R) \Rightarrow D.$$

Again, this emphasizes how C leads to R and back and forth. Calm opens the door for receptivity, and the capacity for receptivity directly influences how much D, or direction, you can provide. But we'll get to that in a moment.

Receptive is a state of mind that can be evoked. In clinical practice, psychologists are taught to create what is alternately referred to as

- rapport,
- alliance,
- coherence, or
- collaboration.

Basically it is the equivalent of when Joan Rivers used to say, "Can we talk?" In operation, this means that at least enough of the receptive systems of the teen are parent focused. This good-enough attention, however, is often defeated by parental emphasis upon being *directive*, our *D* word. For the most part, the road to hellish encounters with teens is paved by placing the cart of directives before the horse of receptivity. Parents, from a teen's perspective, announce commands without attention to their audience. So let's speak of what "directive" means.

> When a parent arrives home, unloads the kids from the car, and then announces that everyone should get in the house, put his or her stuff away, change his or her school clothes, do his or her homework, and not eat anything because supper is early, the parent is providing directives. Let's make it just a little more complicated by saying that while the parent's intention is to provide directive(s), the response of the recipients—the kids—will tell you whether it was a directive or just noise. Philosophically, a directive becomes a directive only when the recipients respond; otherwise it is just noise.

With our scene above, based upon grooming and training and the historical relationship with the children, our parent will either bask in obedience—that is, a response to the directives—or find a kid eating a Fudgsicle melting onto the front of her school shirt while updating her Facebook status and declaring that her homework is done, though it is not! The biggest mistake parents make is only using directives and then lamenting that the kids treat them like noise. Therefore, our next admonition is for fewer directives and more conversation.

CONVERSATION > DIRECTION

Parents always tell kids to come to them with questions or problems or when they want to talk and so on, but they never practice talking or, in a more formal sense, set the context for talking to happen. By "practice" and "set the context," I am suggesting parents talk to their kids in the following ratio of five to one:

> five things that are fun, inconsequential, exciting, mischievous, encouraging, support, cooperative, noncontingent, rewarding, and so on,
> for every one "have you / will you / did you / when / where / what / why" message.

Learn to "waste time conscientiously" with kids in order to create the environment for conscientious attention to the real things that matter when they arise. Before one can talk influence, direction, or authority, one must be able to talk! When we examine the shift from early childhood to teen years, there is a change from more rich, varied, and broad verbal interaction with children to more instrumental/sanctioning communication. By "instrumental" or "sanctioning," I mean directive demands, again our "have you / did you / do / what / when / where / how / why" sorts of invectives.

When parents first begin to wrap themselves around this idea of receptivity and launch into the five-to-one practices, they are often stunned—like the old married couple—to find they don't have much to say to each other! Parent-teen communication has become restricted like a bad diet, to quick, interrogative, directive, and "fast-food" focused interchanges. Teens are more receptive when communication is not restricted and they don't know what is coming. In the restricted range of "have you / did you / what / when" and so on, there is a knee-jerk shutdown at the very sound of the parent's voice as opposed to the quizzical look that arises, tinged with suspicion, when a parent says for the first time, "Hey, do you think pot today is a lot stronger than when I smoked it?"

Receptivity then needs to be cultivated, and the fertilizer is the five-to-one and conscientiously wasting time in conversation. Remember, talk to talk, not to address your needs or anxiety.

But what about those moments when you do need to get something across? How might we foster receptivity in vivo—that instance when we need it? Before we explore this, think back on what you have read and answer the questions as best as you can.

5, 4, 3, 2, 1…

OK, with that in mind, let's move on to some boots on the ground. We know that there are times when we need a specific skill beyond patience, calm(er), and so on. One such skill is the use of other *D* words.

The use of this technique is not limited to adolescents and in fact is the most basic skill for younger children, as well.

D words include such actions as these:

- deflate
- detour
- dilute
- disappear
- divest
- depotentiate
- distract
- dissipate
- decenter

These actions are hand in glove to our earlier terms "engagement," "receptivity," and "calm(er)." It is the use of words to control process, not content. When a parent says to me, "What am I supposed to do when a kid is yelling and swearing at me?" I answer in two ways:

1) Well, let's backtrack so I can see what happened before the yelling, before the swearing or related stomping about.
2) Ah, stop talking. End the conversation. Withdraw. Let it cool down. And so on.

Parents always want to know what to do when the car has gone off the road. This analogy of a vehicle is useful. It is as if you are driving and understand that there is a gas pedal and brakes. As you are moving—in the encounter—there is a tendency toward acceleration. What starts in the mind of an adult is an open, straight road—"We just have to speak about you and your fights with siblings, that schoolwork, your room," and so on. However, in trying to impose authority or control upon the conversation or the teen, the matter accelerates. Velocity—intensity and stronger emotion—increases, and then come the curves or bends in the road, and one or another specific turn isn't negotiated well, and bam! Through the highway guardrail they go! Parents often tell me, "I did what you said," but what they really did was pump the brakes after the rail, when they were in free fall to the bottom of the cliff! Message? Hit the brakes soon, use them more subtly, and often even on a treacherous road, discussion with a teen can be negotiated.

And sometimes it is necessary to just stop the vehicle and pull over to the side of the road. This is hard for parents to understand, for once in free fall—or hell as per the earlier diagram—it seems ludicrous to give in, let them win, do whatever they want then, and so on. This "doing something by not doing something" is very hard for parents and impossible once the interchange has gone to hell. The feelings of impotence and catastrophe associated with putting aside a useless conversation are in fact aspects of the very process we are trying to control. A fight with a teen, or anyone, who is full of self-righteous, negative, confrontational, and demeaning use of strong emotion ("bullying") is not useful and, more to the point, useless and harmful. Even where a parent "wins" through intimidation or escalating emotion, the outcome is a dangerous lesson:

The person with the strongest emotion rules.

Whether pathos or anger, self-pity or aggression, these emotions ought not govern one's own behavior or that of others. So the first rule to teen soothing is to know when a conversation is over and must be put aside. "Put aside" is important, for it means not that the issue is done but that the management of the issue is not timely at this moment. The first time a son or daughter comes home under the influence, most parents know that moment is not the time for the lecture/discussion on intoxicants. (My father would wait until sunrise the next morning to gently but persistently have a few words with us.)

However, all is not lost, and retreat from the field of combat is not our only option, only our fail-safe if exercised in a timely sense. The message then here is this:

> Know when a conversation is over and you are just rolling/tumbling in hell.

If we are clever and can see that we are being coaxed toward hell, we dilute our conversation. By "dilution" I would suggest adding more perspective, sympathy, empathy, and interest and getting closer to the subject.

One last word on something introduced earlier: the difference between content and process. Content means what we are talking about; process means how we are doing it. An argument can be about anything—school, peers, behavior in the home or in the community, and so on. This content is ironically irrelevant. Anything can be spoken of with kids if we can do it in the best way—even sex, drugs, and rock and roll. Process focuses upon the how.

For example, "How are you?"

In a content sense, this is fairly explicit: a common pleasantry associated with conversational greeting. However, cut to another scene and add things such as (1) icy contempt or (2) quick, uninterested urgency or (3) penetrating, compassionate engagement. This constitutes process, the way our comments are dressed, so to speak.

Families have the same kinds of challenges with adolescents but not the same kinds of problems. The difference between the family where the kid is not attending to schoolwork and it has to be addressed and the family where this becomes a problem is the difference in process each family employs. Parents make a mistake, then, in addressing only content; they escalate, introducing variations on the theme: "You need a good education." "What will happen if you do your job like you do school?" "If you're not going to school, then you need to get a job." "You can't live here if you don't assume your responsibilities." The list goes on. This content emphasis becomes litigious, like two lawyers:

- If it pleases the court, I would point out the reluctance to take responsibility for his schoolwork bodes poorly for his future vocational horizons, not to speak of potential difficulty in his current residence.
- In response to my friends, I would point out that they have failed to consider the problems in the character of my teachers and the fact the work involved can always be made up, and perhaps most importantly, that they are unduly anxious sorts of parents!

Process then involves attention to the clothes the conversation is wearing. The ability to dress for the event is critical. Manage, alter, or control process, and you control the world—well, you at least have a little more control with your kids.

CHAPTER 6
Nudging

THE ESSENCE OF CHANGE, LEARNING, or correction is in successive approximations to desired outcome. What this means is a gradual but progressive shift, accomplished in repeated small nudges. By "nudges" I mean inducements to change. An example of a nudge is reflected in the two statements below.

1) Hey, how many times do I have to tell you to hang your jacket up?
2) Hey, I am sorry I forgot to remind you to hang up your jacket.

Subtle, eh? But with the reasoned state of mind we are advocating, it can be an effective, small step:

- Oh, I was supposed to go over your homework with you!
- Can I help you with getting that trash out?
- I'm really glad you got it about getting enough sleep.
- Everyone knows that most kids work out how to manage time.
- Hey, can you either get in your pajamas now and come back down, or just go to bed?
- Hey, would you like to straighten your room up now or after you get the trash out?

The essence of the nudge is a mindless motivation. Think of it: in our own lives, there are things—as there are in the teen lives around us—that we just don't do or won't do because we have been nudged over the years toward or away from certain behaviors. This issue of motivation and positive reinforcement is pretty important. If each conversation is about who is right, efficacious, or competent, who makes decisions, and so on, we are not getting far. If there can be an "atta boy/atta girl" thrown in, the organism can be nudged toward a more calm/receptive status and the behavior we hope for.

The nudge, however, doesn't work or seems pretty anemic when

1) we are already close to hell or heading that way most of the time, or
2) a kid and a parent have already developed a rigid push-pull posture with each other.

Rapid or chronic escalation has to do with knee-jerk reactions to each other's presence and tone of voice. Default to tense confrontation is the norm accompanied by these thoughts:

In the parent's head: "This is going to be another one of those 'here we go agains,' and s/he is just going to do what s/he wants and ignore me, and I will again feel like an impotent servant to a graceless tyrant!"
In the kid's head: "Why are they always on my back and trying to control me and make me do stuff they want? Can't they do it nicer and better? And anyway I don't have to do everything they tell me to do!"

With these situations of concretized conceptualization, each of the other, I suggest the course of implacable immobility.

Implacable Immobility (IM)
This is useful when it comes to the things that must get done—for example, cutting power to electronics, getting up for school, going to bed for the evening, coming home, and so on. IM is reflected in a calm, resolved, and nondistracted holding to the "I need you to _____."

This posture is the calm directive already discussed on pages 10–15. Go back and read that, and then imagine you are strapping on armor of confidence and practice!

It is confidence—a feeling of being able to figure out what you need to do—that is a goal with kids. IM is difficult for most of us as the wrath, indifference, and contempt of a teen may emerge. At the risk of being redundant, it is in our capacity to not go there and to manage our own arousal so that things can work out, and we get through it!

CHAPTER 7

Let Them Do the Work
Socratic as Opposed to Pedantic

Let me set the stage: Discussion. The teen is rolling his or her eyes, breathing deeply, looking away, or perhaps countering adult comments with erudite justifications or wise ass remarks. The parent is providing a virtual PowerPoint on why the teen's conduct is unacceptable, providing exposition on everything from consequentialism, utilitarian perspective, and deontological virtue (I look these terms up under "philosophy"), and two days later the conduct is all the same. Repeat.

This emphasis upon directive, content-focused rationality, and argumentation is often a "why don't you / you must" on the parental side met by a "yeah but…" on the teen side. In fact this very process of adult rationality encountering teen emotionality and justification or defensiveness, while seemingly logical or even intuitive, provides aid and comfort to the very problem of conflict! The more a parent confronts a teen with even the most rational perspectives, unappreciated by the teen, the more the teen gets to practice argumentation and employs his or her rationalization and justification toward the very end the parent wants to confront. See the discussion of process versus content in chapter 5 and the example below:

> Parent: You can't keep on fighting with your sibling.
> Teen: Yeah, but they started it.
> Parent: You are the eldest and should be able to be more mature.
> Teen: You always take their side and treat me different.
> Parent: No, I don't! I am fair to all of you.
> Teen: Then why don't you tell them to behave and quit being such jerks?
> Parent: Don't call you brother and sister names. There's the problem!
> Teen: Well, they are jerks, and if you and Dad could see that, you would discipline them too and not just pick on me and give everything to them and spoil them.
> Parent: Didn't I just buy you all new hockey stuff?

And now the teen has learned more how to employ analytical competency in service to emotional ends that, like a cheap lawyer, can explain away or make a case for anything! Rather than increasing reflection in self-involving accountability, rational basis has now been seconded to immature self-justification and blaming of others.

Responsibility is often the lament of the parents: "He/she has to take responsibility." Responsibility arises from better emotional regulation and self-reflection. So what is our formula to make this a possibility? Hint: It is not the case example above!

With the above we see what deep thinkers refer to as a pedantic discussion—a point-by-point review of a matter. In opposition I propose a modified Socratic discussion. By framing questions or structuring an encounter in specified ways, learning is possible. Socrates proved this to his friend Menro when he showed how an "ignorant" slave boy could master complex geometry. Here is how it works.

First, it is fair to say "Quit fighting with your siblings" to a receptive and responsible teen. However, where the pattern above is likely or probable, the move is to a Socratic posture. This involves creating some calmer receptivity (CR) and then an inquiry where the teen does the heavy lifting. The basis with our example is the question "Why is there a problem with this sibling-fighting stuff?" Now it is incredibly important to understand this is not a "corner the kid" endeavor. Most teens go silent or sulk when asked questions of this sort because they are sure the parent will throw their answers back in their faces. If you ask "Why a problem?" and then use the response to indict, you have missed the point:

Parent: Can you tell me why sibling fighting is a problem?
Teen: Well, it makes the family a tense place.
Parent: Ah, so you admit that it's a problem!

Teens expect that any discussion of frankness or vulnerability will lead to censorship or self-incrimination, so either dissociate—take the

Fifth through silent nonengagement—or proceed to do what I describe above. The Socratic method needs to be something different and goes like this:

> Parent: Hey, this stuff with your siblings is not right.
> Teen: Yeah, but…
> Parent: Yeah, I know they are a challenge, but can you give me two or three reasons this kind of stuff can be a problem?
> Teen: It's not my fault. They start it.
> Parent: No, yeah, I get it, but I'm just asking why this might or could be a problem.
> Teen: You need to punish them.
> Parent: Yeah, probably, but wait, just give me a few reasons why this is not good.
> Teen: Well, we get in trouble.
> Parent: Ah, for sure that makes sense, but why is trouble bad?
> Teen: Well, you guys then are always yelling.
> Parent: For sure, the parents become offensive and difficult. Keep it rolling.
> Teen: We lose privileges and get punished.
> Parent: Nice move, for sure freedom gets restricted. Bonus round! Go for some more.
> Teen: Well, you treat me worse.
> Parent: For sure it can affect the way we think about you, but why is that important?
> Teen: Well, I want you guys to like me, at least respect me.
> Parent: You are on fire. This sibling stuff can make us an unhappy family, you're the guy in trouble, it takes away fun, it creates a bad image of our kids, and one more?
> Teen: Huh? What?
> Parent: Well, it can make parents feel like they don't do a good job.
> Teen: Ah!

The point is a theoretical discussion about the potential problems with the issue of school, fighting at home, smoking pot, and so on: no attribution, judgement, or specifics involved in service to—you guessed it!—more reflective, broader analysis. This "let's see why something might be a problem" approach moves from defense on the part of the teen and retreat from useless lecture by the parent to nonjudgmental dialogue.

In clinical practice and even with parents, I use a reward system. Specifically in my office, when a parent issues a complaint and the teen defends, I often proceed with the Socratic method. This involves asking the teen why this situation could or might be a problem. I keep a handful of coins available and say I will pay a dollar for every reason he or she can imagine. My record is nine dollars for an initially sullen, reluctant kid whose answers on the topic of coming home on time ranged from domestic tranquility through reflections upon his character to concern for the impact of his conduct upon the endurance of his parents' marriage. I have suggested a parent say/use, "Punishment may be put off if you can give me three reasons, potentially, for why this behavior could or might be a problem."

There is a strong rationale for this as the contemplation by the teen is rehearsal for improved behavior. Not only is the teen practicing using those reflective, analytical parts of his or her brain, but he or she is creating potential self-directives and, as with my example above, doing so in an engaged more calm/receptive state of mind.

CHAPTER 8
Punishment? (The Shortest Chapter in the Book)

PARENTS HAVE OFTEN SAID THAT now that their children are teens, they are too old/big to punish, meaning the kids can resist or, worse, fight back. In this statement is the whole argument.

Punishment is to stop a behavior or prevent it by force of one sort or another. However, punishment is not associated with the sort of second-order learning we are speaking about here:

- First-order learning by a kid is to not get caught, because you get punished.
- Second-order learning is how to behave to avoid situations related to confrontation or punishment.

So punishment is really about something else. For a parent, punishment is the pursuit of authority. When feeling out of control—without agency or authority—a parent can get it back real quick with yelling or the swinging of a hand. So punishment is about you more often than the child.

What is punishment, then, in the context of this approach? The disappointment of or rejection by a figure of authority whom you respect.

"I just never wanted to let my mom/dad down" is probably the best way to think of kinetic or potential punishment a kid would fear—and one you can use, if you've taken the time to practice what this book preaches.

CHAPTER 9
Some Final Encouragement

WE ARE ALWAYS DOING THE best we can with the demands that exist around us in this crazy, multifaceted, multiversal situation we call modern life. If we could teleport our great-grandparents to a day in the life most of us live, they would no doubt see more insanity than sanity. In our lives it is as if we are on treadmill; no matter how fast we run, the promised place of "it's all good" is never achieved. This sense of "just around the corner, it will all be good, settled, resolved, and so on" is reflected in the urgency associated with this sentiment:

> If I can just get them up, dressed, fed, off to school, and dropped off, and I can just get to work and pick them up, grab the groceries, get them organized to do their homework, off to extracurricular activities, and then home, fed, and set time for bed and settled down, I could…

This hedonic treadmill related to "just around the corner" is ubiquitous to North American life for most of us. It's not your fault then; it isn't because you are not as good, or not good enough, or behind the others. None of us are the others! So perhaps the prescription here is one of quiet rebellion, probably the only hope we really have. As key to this series of thought experiments described above—experiments intended to alter your state of mind—I would add one more final encouragement. It is useful to see the teen years the same way we might see someone recovering from an unfortunate accident, someone learning to walk again or feed himself or herself or struggling with regaining muscular strength—an acute but recovery-focused and optimistic medical condition.

As with medical recovery, there will be good days and bad days. On the good days, we celebrate and share in the accomplishments, whether walking a few steps, being able to get up/down stairs, or feeding oneself. This is the positive reinforcement the manuals talk about, not a salacious "reward" but the real joy in disciplined, self-monitored responsibility. On the other hand, the off days are seen less as opportunity but rather a time to offer support and encouragement: "The walking will come," "You'll get your energy back," or "It's just going to take time." While the teen may need nudges or confrontation when seen through this medical lens, we offer such from a better state of mind. Rather than see the bad days as failed adult standards, we can appreciate the struggle associated with adult recovery and approximation. No one yells at a guy who falls off his crutches, eh?

With this in mind, I will sign off. There is a lot more that can be said about kids, and has been. There is also more to these ideas than just their relation to teens; they work with difficult spouses, younger kids, and even difficult coworkers!

Central to the principles here, however, is the old adage "Be the change here you would seek there." As Eminem once said, "Can't do something [we] didn't teach them." Hence rather than simple compliance to our needs, situation to situation, what we are after is a more global shift in relational emphasis. If you truly decide to not lose your mind, the joy of the teen as opportunity emerges.

Made in the USA
Charleston, SC
27 November 2016